TABLE OF CONTENTS

The Complete Slow Cooker Keto Diet Recipe Book

Quick and Delicious Keto Diet Recipes for Your Slow Cooker incl. 28-Day Weight Loss Plan

Sarah H. Graham

ISBN- 9798697643235

INTRODUCTION

If you're new, welcome to the ketogenic diet! We hope to explain how and why this innovative new diet works, and how it may benefit you with your health, wellbeing and weight-loss goals.

We understand the day to day struggle finding a successful and sustainable diet plan that suits your busy lifestyle.

Read on to discover the basic principles of a Ketogenic diet, who it's for and how it works.

In this book we've specifically compiled a selection of delicious, simple recipes designed for your slow cooker. Keto just got even easier!

This no nonsense diet is based around delicious homemade meals and fresh, local ingredients. Wave goodbye to the days of microwavable ready-meals, replacement shakes and monotonous gym workouts. Keto is here to stay.

Traditionally, the majority of 'old fashioned' diet plans were bland, restrictive and costly - leaving you feeling lethargic, frustrated and craving all the 'forbidden' food you're not allowed to eat.

We also know how unmotivating it is when you step on the scales every week and don't see any progress. All that work for nothing! Well, worry not. Struggling to stick to that tiny and soul crushing daily calorie intake is now a thing of the past. The ketogenic diet could be what you've been searching for all this time.

With these slow cooker recipes you have the ability to prepare your meals well in advance, or even the night before. Simply pop your keto-friendly meal in the slow cooker, switch it on, go to bed and wake up to the delicious smell of breakfast in the morning. No more setting alarms early to prepare packed lunches, or getting home from a tiring day at work to immediately have to make dinner for the kids... everything can now be prepared to suit your schedule.

This Ketogenic diet is backed up by science and years of trials and research. They've finally worked out the answers to healthy, quick, safe and sustainable weight loss, all from the comfort of your own home. Too good to be true, you ask? It's really quite simple, trust us, you will notice results after 28 days guaranteed with the help of our tasty slow-cooker keto recipes, complete with nutritional information and portion guidelines, there's even a bonus 28-day meal plan at the end of this book!

The advantages of using a slow-cooker:

For a lot of people trying to lose weight, constantly cooking and being in the kitchen is the last thing you feel like doing after a hard day at work.

Planning meals and spending hours in the kitchen every day can be draining and push people to give in to temptation and order a take-away instead.

Using a slow-cooker means you can prepare meals when it suits you, be it in the morning while you wait for the kids to get ready for school, your lunch break during work, or even in the evenings before you go to bed. A slow cooker gives you so much more control and flexibility, and ensures there's always healthy and delicious keto-friendly food at your fingertips.

This method of slow cooking seals in all the flavour, nutrition and good fats. Not to mention always creating the most delicious, juicy and tender meats, stews and soups. Even if you don't have much in the fridge, you can create a tasty meal with basic ingredients in no time, switch on the slow cooker and get on with your day knowing your homemade dinner is covered.

There is also the added advantage of being able to save space in your kitchen, reduce mess and washing up. Giving you extra time to relax or pursue your favorite hobbies.

You can cook everything directly from frozen which also saves time and means you don't have to remember to get your meat out of the freezer in advance. Just simply place everything into the slow cooker, turn it on, adjust the temperature and set the timer. Walk away and get on with your day, knowing that your meal will be ready when you need it to be.

What is the keto diet?

The basic principles of a ketogenic diet are very simple. Maintaining a very low sugar, low carbohydrate diet, while subsidising with very high-fat, medium protein meals instead.

In many ways, the Ketogenic diet is similar to the well known classic, The Atkins Diet. It differs however, by focusing on healthier natural fats, fresh vegetables and protein.

We now have the science to back up why sugars and simple carbohydrates can lead to problems with glucose regulation in the blood, weight gain, and feeling sluggish and fatigued.

The ketogenic diet works by:

 - dramatically increasing 'good' fat consumption

 - maintaining average or medium protein intake

 - eating fewer carbohydrates substantially

How does the keto diet work?

A dramatic and sudden reduction in carbohydrates and sugars will push your body into an important metabolic state called 'ketosis'.

Ketosis means that your body begins to use fat rather than sugar (glucose) as its main source of energy.

Basically a controlled form of starvation, the ketogenic diet tricks your body into burning fat stored in the body, together with the fat consumed in your diet, as fuel instead of carbohydrates and sugars.

This aids very fast, efficient and maintainable weight loss, even without doing any notable bouts of exercise.

When carbohydrates are consumed, the glucose from the food gets stored in the liver and gradually released when required for energy. This works wonderfully, until the carbohydrate intake drops, for example, skipping a meal. The glucose levels in the liver become depleted, at which point we start feeling cranky and lethargic, or craving sugary, sweet or fatty junk food. Luckily ketosis, once achieved, comes to the rescue as a helpful alternative energy source!

The liver is constantly producing 'Ketone Enzymes' all the time, as a way of keeping us going when our glucose levels are low, such as when we're asleep, intermittent fasting or skipping meals when we are busy. The ketones are efficient but only do the job for as long as they are required, as soon as we consume carbohydrates again the liver switches back to running on sugar (glucose) as its main 'fuel source'.

However, when dramatically reducing carbohydrate intake for a prolonged amount of time, usually 4 or 5 days, we can enter the metabolic state known as 'nutritional ketosis' - This means that your liver is producing a sufficient amount of ketones to keep you running throughout the day without any carbohydrates or sugar at all!

Because our body is so efficient at storing 'fat' it rarely runs out of this new energy source. Ketones continue burning fat as energy and this is how we notice such a quick and easy weight-loss journey. Once in 'nutritional ketosis' you'll notice your energy levels stay the same, your mind will be clearer and more focused and you won't experience waves of hunger or irritability as these feelings are directly linked to the body needing a top up of carbohydrates to continue running. When in ketosis, you'll notice you no-longer crave food or feel the need to snack as much. You may even find that you feel better from intermittent fasting.

Who is this diet for?

The Keto Diet is suitable for everyone! It's principles are simple and easy to follow.

Why not give it a go today and start your weight-loss journey today.

This book 'Quick and Delicious Keto Diet Recipes for Your Slow Cooker incl. 28-Day Weight Loss Plan' makes it even more achievable, with our detailed list of slow-cooker friendly recipes, cooking instructions and extensive 28-day weight loss plan.

Scientists studying ketosis have made some amazing health discoveries over the years.

Research now shows that just 4-weeks of a strict 'nutritional ketosis' can improve symptoms of pre-diabetes, type 2 diabetes, hormonal imbalances, migraine headaches, polycystic ovaries, calm children with ADHD, assist in seizure management for people suffering with epilepsy and potentially even slow down the devastating effects of Alzheimers on the brain!

Like any new diet, we always recommend you consult your doctor beforehand and have a basic health-check before undertaking any dramatic change to your diet or routine.

Whilst proven to be safe, the ketogenic diet is extreme and needs to be approached with caution. If you have diabetes, thyroid problems, cancer, high blood pressure, a history of heart disease or stroke, or if you are pregnant or breastfeeding or have food allergies, it's best to seek the opinion of a qualified medical professional. Likewise, always notify your doctor if you are feeling unwell after starting a ketogenic diet - it's better to be safe than sorry.

Why is the keto diet so successful?

The beauty of a ketogenic diet is the way it changes your mind-set and relationship with food.

Even though it is hard initially or for the first time, the process of ditching carbohydrates and getting through the 'keto flu' phase becomes easier and easier till you hardly notice the irritability or cravings associated with quitting carbohydrates and sugar.

While the keto-diet is not considered a long term or sustainable way of eating forever, you can 'carb cycle' and dip in and out of ketosis every couple of months to reap the benefits on your weight and health! It's amazing to feel so light, full of energy and focused on the day ahead.

You'll notice your relationship with food changing after the first couple of weeks on a Ketogenic Diet - Making good food choices will start to come naturally, and the guilt surrounding high fat or high protein foods disappears. Counting calories and feeling guilt and shame for indulging in fatty foods such as cheese or double cream disappear - Just because keto is labeled as a 'diet' doesn't mean you can't enjoy your food!

The established advantages and benefits of a ketogenic diet are as follows:

> ❧ **A reduced and more regulated appetite throughout the day:** When initially going into the 'ketogenic state' it can be a shock to the

body and leave you feeling deflated and frustrated - This is known as 'keto flu', when you experience cravings and irritability. These are common side effects of low glucose levels but will subside after a few days! Once in 'nutritional ketosis', one of the first things people notice is that they no longer feel hungry or crave food like they used too. Scientific trials have proven that being in ketosis suppresses your appetite substantially. It's a lot easier to ditch the extra pounds when we're not craving all the 'forbidden' foods.

- **Rapid weight loss:** Once in the 'nutritional ketosis' state, your body will shift to burning fat as its main fuel source. This ability to use stored fat as energy to keep you going throughout the day, combined with a dramatically reduced appetite, means many people notice the kg's dropping off in a matter of weeks. The beauty of ketosis is that you don't even need to count calories, waste time on an arduous workout routine or essentially torture your mind with starving yourself to achieve weight-loss.

- **A better, steady supply of energy and improved focus:** Once your body has made the switch from running on gluten to ketones, you will notice you suddenly feel lighter, less hungry, less irritable and can focus on things better. That brain fog has lifted and food is no longer number one priority. Many people notice their performance at school, work or the gym improves dramatically after the 2nd week of ketosis. Children on a high fat and protein diet, especially for breakfast, appear to do better at school and have more focus in the classroom than compared with children that consume high-sugar high-carbohydrate breakfasts such as cereal or toast with jam. It suddenly becomes so much easier to get on with your day to day activities and that is why the ketogenic diet is so easy to maintain!

☙ **A noticeable improvement, or even reversal of pre-diabetes and type 2- diabetes:** It has been observed in scientific trials with diabetic patients who are following a strict low-carbohydrate diet can help 'normalise' their blood sugar and insulin regulation in the blood, potentially reversing some of the damage that can be caused by pre-diabetes. If maintained and carefully monitored, the ketogenic diet can actually lead to no longer having to take daily diabetes medication.

Useful tips for when you're feeling unmotivated, or struggling to enter Ketosis:

☙ **A high-fat diet isn't bad:** It is essential that you are consuming a substantial amount of fat whilst on a ketogenic diet. This is where your body is getting all of its fuel from after-all! If you're worried about 'bad' fats, you can try and incorporate more plant-based, 'healthier' fats such as olive oil, nuts, avocado and coconut cream into your diet plan.

- **Try regular intermittent fasting:** Have a go at intermittent fasting! At the beginning, when initially trying to enter 'nutritional ketosis' it can be difficult to give up the snack foods or stick to such a high fat-low carb diet! You can kick start the ketosis transition quicker by intermittent fasting. Going without food for 12-15 hours can be really daunting, but you only need to do it right at the beginning to kick-start a quick and easy transition from running on glucose to ketones. It can be as easy as skipping breakfast and then eating an early dinner!

- **Plan, plan, plan:** Having a diet plan is essential for keeping up with your weight-loss goals! In this handy book we have included a great little 28-day meal plan with breakfast, lunch, dinner, snacks and desserts. Doing one big weekly shop is often quicker and easier, and helps you get your meal prepping done in advance. Nipping to the shops constantly or every couple of days can tempt you to splash out on snacks, deals or impulse buys that don't help us with maintaining ketosis! We recommend you plan your meal's out week by week, make a list and get everything you need in one go! Making meals in your slow cooker has never been easier, and many of our recipes in this book are for 4-6 portions - enough to feed the whole family or keep in the fridge and eat throughout the week!

- **Reduce your daily 'net-carb' consumption:** The sooner you ditch the carbohydrates and enter ketosis the better you'll feel! Cutting your carbohydrate intake to less than 20 grams of net carbs every day can quickly assist in achieving 'nutritional ketosis', some can start running on ketones as soon as 2-3 days after making the change to their diet! Luckily for you, we've included all the nutritional information and portion sizes in this handy recipe book to get you started!

❧ **Ditch the processed foods:** As tempting as it is, processed foods often contain all kinds of keto no-no's! Hidden away in these processed meats, sauces and packaged foods are often huge quantities of salt, sugar, saturated (bad) fats, glutin, thickeners and artificial flavorings... all of which are likely to kick you out of ketosis in a flash, before you've even noticed! It's important to go back to basics when beginning a ketogenic diet - Try and source organic whole vegetables and meat or fish from the butchers or deli counter in your supermarket! Beware of cheap salami's or sausages as these usually contain the most keto 'nasties' such as flour (glutin) as a binding agent! If in doubt, always read the label and try and minimise your net carbohydrate intake to less than 20g each day.!

❧ **There's no need to count calories:** It's difficult to go against all the dietary advice you've ever been given, but trust us! It can be hard to get your head round, but calories don't mean anything when it comes to the ketogenic diet! We strongly recommend that you throw caution to the wind and turn a blind eye to the calorie count of each meal, especially at the beginning while you retrain your brain! It is essential to getting enough fats, after all this is the new fuel you'll be running on.

&❧ **Dining out on Keto:** It's important to not let this diet rule your life! Dining out on keto can be a real treat, you just need to follow a few basic rules! Firstly, choose your drinks carefully. Avoid fruit juices, sweet cocktails or dark spirits. It's okay to drink alcohol on keto, just make sure you choose 'dry wines' and 'white spirits' with soda water or sugar free mixers! Try and eliminate the starch and choose healthy fats and protein instead - Ask the waiter to replace the burger bun with salad for example! Try and plan in advance and choose what you want to eat before you get to the restaurant. Most p;aces have menus online these days luckily, or you can ask your friends or work colleagues. Go easy on sauces and condiments too, there's a surprising amount of sugar in tomato ketchup for example! Likewise, say no to sugary desserts and opt for the cheese board instead. The ketogenic diet is becoming a well-known and respected diet and many restaurants are happy to cater for the keto-conscious customer! Let your waiter know when you make the reservation and they are usually more than happy to accommodate your dietary requirements!

We've compiled '*The Complete Keto Diet Recipe Book - Quick and Delicious Keto Diet Recipes for Your Slow Cooker incl. 28-Day Weight Loss Plan*' for you to enjoy a wide range of mouth watering keto recipes for your breakfast, lunch, dinner, snacks and desserts, all written with simple instructions, ingredients, measurements, portion sizes and nutritional information!

This book should be enough to get you started on your health and weight-loss journey! After completing the 28-day meal plan you could even get creative and use some of the other recipes in this book to create your own tailor-made meal plan for months and months to come! Try changing the seasonings in some sauces, or swap the meat for fish or tofu?

The possibilities are endless and there's no time like the present to get started. What are you waiting for? The ketogenic diet could be your fast ticket to feeling great and ditching those stubborn extra-pounds!

BREAKFAST

Keto Coconut Porridge

Net carbs: 4g / Fibre: 5g / Fat: 64g / Protein: 12g / Calories: 642
Prep time: 5 min / Cooking time: 6 hours / Servings: 1 / Serving size: 1 cup

INGREDIENTS:

- 1tbsp chia seeds
- 1tbsp sesame seeds
- 1 egg

- 75ml // ⅓ cup coconut cream
- 30g // 1oz coconut oil
- Pinch of salt

METHOD:

1. Weigh out all of the ingredients and mix together in the bottom of your slow cooker.

2. Cook overnight on the lowest setting, approximately 5-6 hours.

3. Serve with fresh fruit like blueberries or raspberries.

Bacon and Egg Breakfast Slice

Net carbs: 1g / Fibre: 0g / Fat: 11g / Protein: 16g / Calories: 171
Prep time: 5 min / Cooking time: 4 hours / Servings: 3 / Serving size: 1

INGREDIENTS:

- ♦ 75g // 3oz streaky bacon
- ♦ 75g // 3oz grated cheddar cheese
- ♦ 6 large eggs
- ♦ Pinch of salt and pepper

METHOD:

1. Chop the strips of bacon in half and use them to line the bottom of your greased slow cooker.

2. Whisk the eggs with half of the cheese and season well. Pour the mixture into the bacon lined slow cooker.

3. Grate the remaining cheese on top and cook on a medium temperature for 4 hours. Cut into slices and serve.

Spanish Breakfast Tortillas

Net carbs: 1g / Fibre: 1g / Fat: 15g / Protein: 13g / Calories: 162
Prep time: 5 min / Cooking time: 3 hours / Servings: 3 / Serving size: 1

INGREDIENTS:

- 75g // 3oz grated cheddar cheese
- 3 large onions
- 6 large eggs
- Pinch of salt and pepper

METHOD:

1. Slice the onion thinly and set aside.

2. Whisk the eggs, cheese and seasoning together, mix in the sliced raw onion.

3. Pour everything into your greased slow cooker pot and cook for 4 hours on a medium heat.

4. Slice and serve.

Stewed Summer Berries with Yoghurt

Net carbs: 6g / Fibre: 5g / Fat: 29g / Protein: 3g / Calories: 307
Prep time: 5 min / Cooking time: 2 hours / Servings: 2 / Serving size: 1

INGREDIENTS:

- 150g // 5oz fresh berries, such as raspberries, strawberries or blueberries
- 1 tsp cinnamon
- 1 lemon, zest and juice
- 150ml // ⅔ cup yoghurt

METHOD:

1. Place the berries, lemon juice, zest and the cinnamon into your slow cooker and gently stew on a low temperature for 2 hours.

2. Once cooked, chill the fruit compote in the fridge overnight. Serve with a dollop of full fat greek yoghurt in the morning as a quick and simple breakfast.

Sausage and Egg Bake

Net carbs: 9g / Fibre: 2g / Fat: 67g / Protein: 51g / Calories: 543
Prep time: 5 min / Cooking time: 3 hours / Servings: 4 / Serving size: 1

INGREDIENTS:

- 500g // 1lb good quality, gluten-free pork sausages
- 6 eggs
- 6 button mushrooms
- 6 cherry tomatoes
- 2tbsp butter
- Fresh parsley
- Salt and pepper

METHOD:

1. Slice the cherry tomatoes and mushrooms in halves or quarters.

2. Grease the slow cooker pan with the butter, place the sausages down first, then sprinkle the chopped tomatoes and mushrooms on top.

3. Lastly, gently crack the eggs into the gaps around the sausages, keeping the yolks intact. Season with salt and pepper and cook for 3 hours at medium slow cooker temperature.

Breakfast Shakshuka

Net carbs: 7g / Fibre: 4g / Fat: 38g / Protein: 31g / Calories: 504
Prep time: 5 min / Cooking time: 3 hours / Servings: 6 / Serving size: 1

INGREDIENTS:

- 500g // 1lb chorizo sausage
- 75g // 3oz grated cheese
- 1 onion
- 6 large eggs
- 1 small courgette
- 2 tins chopped tomatoes
- 1 large red pepper
- 4 garlic cloves
- ½ tsp chilli powder
- ½ tsp paprika
- ½ tsp cumin
- ½ black pepper
- 1 tsp salt
- Fresh parsley for garnishing

METHOD:

1. Slice and dice the chorizo sausage, onion, pepper and courgettes.

2. Place in your slow cooker, sprinkle over all of the seasoning, herbs and spices and pour over the tinned tomatoes. Stir gently to incorporate everything.

3. Bake for 2 hours at a high heat in your slow cooker. Then remove the lid and using the back of a spoon, make 6 little wells in your sauce.

4. Crack the eggs into each well, sprinkle over the cheese and replace the lid.

5. Bake for a further 1 hour to let the eggs poach and the cheese melt. Serve with a sprinkle of fresh parsley.

Scrambled Tofu with Chives

Net carbs: 2g / Fibre: 5g / Fat: 17g / Protein: 35g / Calories: 281
Prep time: 5 min / Cooking time: 2 hours / Servings: 2 / Serving size: 1

INGREDIENTS:

- ◆ 375g // 13oz tofu
- ◆ ¼ tsp ground turmeric
- ◆ 1 tbsp nutritional yeast powder
- ◆ 175ml // ¾ cup soy milk
- ◆ 2tbsp garlic chives, chopped

METHOD:

1. Crumble the tofu directly into your slow cooker.

2. Pour over the soy milk, salt, pepper, turmeric and nutritional yeast. Stir gently to combine.

3. Cook at a low heat for 2 hours. Gently stir again before serving, and sprinkle the chopped chives on top!

Courgette Breakfast Loaf with Butter

Net carbs: 1g / Fibre: 1g / Fat: 5g / Protein: 4g / Calories: 73
Prep time: 10 min / Cooking time: 2 hours / Servings: 20 / Serving size: 1

INGREDIENTS:

- 400g // 14 oz courgette
- 6 eggs
- 100g // 1 cup grated cheese
- 60g // ½ cup almond meal
- 35g // ¼ cup sunflower seeds
- 2tbsp ground psyllium husk powder
- 2 tsp baking powder
- 1tsp dried rosemary
- 1tbsp poppy seeds
- Salt and pepper

METHOD:

1. Coarsely grate the courgette and place in a bowl. Crack the eggs and mix in well.

2. Beat in the grated cheese, almond meal, sunflower seeds, psyllium husk powder, baking powder, rosemary and seasoning. Leave to thicken up for 10 minutes.

3. Grease your slow cooker pan and pour in the courgette bread 'dough'. Sprinkle the top of the bread with poppy seeds and bake at a medium temperature for 3 hours, or until risen and a toothpick comes out clean.

4. Slice your bread once it's cooled down and enjoy with lots of butter for a quick and easy breakfast.

Keto Spiced Chai 'Oatmeal'

Net carbs: 9g / Fibre: 5g / Fat: 33g / Protein: 11g / Calories: 374
Prep time: 2 min / Cooking time: 1 hour / Servings: 2 / Serving size: 1

INGREDIENTS:

- 60g // ½ cup unsweetened coconut
- 40g // ¼ cup hemp seeds
- 1tbsp coconut flour
- 225ml // 1 cup full fat coconut cream
- ½ tsp cinnamon
- 1 tsp vanilla
- ½ tsp ground ginger
- ¼ tsp ground cardamom
- 120g // 1 cup whole almonds (to serve)

METHOD:

1. Mix all of the ingredients together in your slow cooker, gently stir to incorporate.

2. Cook at a low temperature for 1 hour. Serve warm with whole almonds and a sprinkle of extra cinnamon.

Slow Cooker Keto Cinnamon Swirl Cake

Net carbs: 8g / Fibre: 6g / Fat: 22g / Protein: 9g / Calories: 261
Prep time: 5 min / Cooking time: 2 hour / Servings: 8 / Serving size: 1

INGREDIENTS:

Cake:

- ♦ 10 eggs
- ♦ 95g // ¾ cup coconut flour
- ♦ 70g // ½ cup butter
- ♦ 70g // ½ cup flaxseed meal

- ♦ 2tbsp stevia sweetener
- ♦ 1 tbsp gelatin
- ♦ 2tsp vanilla extract

Cinnamon Syrup:

- ♦ 70g // ½ cup butter
- ♦ 1tbsp stevia sweetener

- ♦ 2tsp cinnamon

Cream Cheese Frosting:

- ♦ 225g // 8oz cream cheese
- ♦ 2 tbsp stevia sweetener
- ♦ ½ tsp vanilla extract

METHOD:

1. Beat together all of the cake batter ingredients and pour into your greased slow cooker pot. Bake for 2 hours at a medium temperature, or until a toothpick comes out clean.

2. While the cake bakes, make the cinnamon syrup by melting together all the ingredients. Set to one side.

3. Once the cake is cooked and the slow cooker has been turned off, poke holes in the sponge with a fork and pour over the cinnamon syrup.

4. For the frosting, beat together the cream cheese, sweetener and vanilla extract. Spoon all over the top of your cool cinnamon swirl cake and spread around evenly covering the top of the cake.

5. Enjoy a slice with your morning coffee.

LUNCH

Middle Eastern Slow Cooker Beef

Net Carbs: 1g / Fiber: 5g / Fat: 27g / Protein: 27g / Calories: 372
Prep time: 7 min / Cooking time: 8 hours / Servings: 6 / Serving size: 1 cup

INGREDIENTS:

- 40g // 1 ½ oz onion, sliced
- 900g // 2lb beef joint
- 4tbsp garam masala
- 1tsp cumin
- ½ tsp cinnamon
- 3 cloves of garlic
- 1 tsp salt
- 1tsp ground pepper
- 600ml // 2 ½ cups water

METHOD:

1. Mince the garlic and mix with the garam masala, cumin, cinnamon salt and pepper.

2. Rub the beef joint with the paste and place in the slow cooker.

3. Pour over the water and cook in the slow cooker on a low heat for 8 hours, or overnight.

4. When the meat is cooked, gently shred with two forks and mix in with the leftover liquid.

5. Serve with butter braised cabbage, your favorite green veggies or make it into a wrap with one of our keto flatbread recipes.

BBQ Pulled Pork

Net Carbs: 9g / Fiber: 5g / Fat: 66g / Protein: 29g / Calories: 726
Prep time: 5 min / Cooking time: 6 hours / Servings: 6 / Serving size: 1

INGREDIENTS:

- 30oz // 900g pork shoulder
- 1tbsp // 5g cocoa powder
- ½ tbsp ground black pepper
- 1tbsp salt
- ½ tsp ground ginger
- ½ tsp fennel seeds
- ½ tsp smoked paprika
- ½ tsp cayenne pepper
- 2tbsp olive oil

METHOD:

1. Mix all of the herbs and spices with the oil to form a paste. Rub the meat with the paste and leave to marinate for 1 hour.

2. Cook in your slow cooker for 6 hours on a low temperature until the meat is tender and can be shredded with a fork.

3. Serve drizzled in homemade keto friendly BBQ sauce, salad and coleslaw.

Keto BBQ Sauce

Net Carbs: 6g / Fiber: 2g / Fat: 9g / Protein: 15g / Calories: 50
Prep time: 15 min / Cooking time: 4 hours / Servings: 6 / Serving size: 1

INGREDIENTS:

- 3tbsp olive oil
- 1tbsp tomato paste
- ½ onion, finely minced
- 2tsp garlic powder
- 2tsp fennel seeds
- 1tsp ground cumin

- 1tbsp chilli powder
- ½ tsp cayenne pepper
- 400g // 14oz tinned chopped tomatoes
- 2tbsp cider vinegar
- 2tsp salt

METHOD:

1. Place the minced onion, herbs, spices and seasoning in a bowl and stir to combine. Pour over the chopped tomatoes and the vinegar and mix.

2. Pour into your slow cooker (or directly onto any bbq flavour meat you want to slow cook) and cook at a low heat for 4 hours.

3. Once simmered, pour the sauce into a blender and wizz until smooth and thick. If the sauce is still a little thin it can be added back to the slow cooker pan and simmered for an additional 30 minutes until thicker.

4. This sauce can be kept in the fridge for up to 2 weeks.

Stuffed Bell-Pepper Poppers

Net carbs: 6g / Fibre: 1g / Fat: 37g / Protein: 12g / Calories: 412
Prep time: 5 min / Cooking time: 2 hours / Servings: 4 / Serving size: 1

INGREDIENTS:

- 225g // 8oz small red peppers
- 30g // 1oz chorizo sausage
- 1 tbsp thyme
- 225g // 8oz cream cheese
- ½ tsp tabasco sauce
- 2tbsp olive oil
- 110g // 4oz cheese, grated

METHOD:

1. Slice each pepper in half and carefully remove the seeds.

2. Chop the chorizo sausage into small chunks and mix together with the cream cheese, thyme and tabasco.

3. Use the oil to grease the inside of your slow cooker so the peppers do not stick.

4. Spoon the mixture into each red pepper half, arrange in the bottom of your slow cooker and top with grated cheese.

5. Bake for 2 hours at a high temperature.

Hearty Chicken Soup

Net carbs: 4g / Fibre: 1g / Fat: 40g / Protein: 33g / Calories: 519
Prep time: 10 min / Cooking time: 6 hours / Servings: 8 / Serving size: 1

INGREDIENTS:

- 110g // 4oz butter
- 2tbsp white onion
- 2 celery sticks
- 175g // 6oz mushrooms
- 2 garlic cloves, minced
- 1 bay leaf

- 2l // 8 cups chicken stock
- 1 carrot
- 2tsp dried parsley
- 4 chicken breasts
- 150g // 5oz green cabbage

METHOD:

1. Slice the vegetables and chicken breast into neat little chunks or strips and add to your slow cooker with the butter.

2. Spoon over the dried parsley and bayleaf. Add the stock and cook on a medium temperature for 6 hours.

Warm Broccoli Salad

Net Carbs: 10g / Fiber: 6g / Fat: 21g / Protein: 7g / Calories: 402
Prep time: 2 min / Cooking time: 2 hours / Servings: 4 / Serving size: 1

INGREDIENTS:

- 450g // 1lb broccoli
- 225ml // 1 cup mayonnaise
- 125ml // ½ cup chopped fresh coriander
- Salt and pepper to taste

METHOD:

1. Chop the broccoli into small florets, drizzle in melted butter and bake in your slow cooker for 2 hours.

2. Mix the mayonnaise with the chopped coriander and salt and pepper.

3. Toss the cooked broccoli in the mayonnaise mixture and serve while still warm as an accompaniment to your favorite slow cooker meat dish.

Tuna Steak Cheese Melt

Net Carbs: 5g / Fiber: 3g / Fat: 67g / Protein: 38g / Calories: 787
Prep time: 10 min / Cooking time: 3 hours / Servings: 4 / Serving size: 1

INGREDIENTS:

- 500g // 1lb tuna steaks
- 125g // 4 ½ oz cream cheese
- 275g // 10oz grated cheese
- 50g // 2oz dill pickles

- 1 garlic clove, minced
- ¼ tsp cayenne pepper
- Salt and pepper

METHOD:

1. Mix together the cream cheese, grated cheese, minced garlic and seasoning.

2. Lay the tuna steaks on the bottom of your greased slow cooker pan, place sliced pickles on top of the tuna, then carefully spread the cheesy mixture over the top of each tuna steak. Sprinkle with a little cayenne pepper.

3. Bake in the slow cooker for 3 hours at a medium heat. This is delicious served hot, accompanying a healthy salad or your favorite green vegetables.

Cheesy Philly-Cheesesteak Soup

Net Carbs: 4g / Fiber: 1g / Fat: 24g / Protein: 29g / Calories: 356
Prep time: 10 min / Cooking time: 5 hours / Servings: 6 / Serving size: 1

INGREDIENTS:

- 3tbsp butter
- ½ red onion
- 1 green pepper
- 110g // 4oz mushrooms
- 450g // 1lb roast beef
- 1l // 4 cups beef broth
- 110g // 4oz cream cheese
- 175g // 6oz grated cheese
- Salt and pepper
- Fresh chopped chives for garnishing

METHOD:

1. Thinly slice the pre-cooked roast beef, onion, green pepper and mushrooms.

2. Using the butter, grease the inside of your slow cooker pan. Place all of your chopped ingredients into the pan.

3. Whisk together the hot beef broth, grated cheese and cream cheese. Season well and pour onto the vegetables and beef in your slow cooker.

4. Cook at a low heat for 4-5 hours, until thick and bubbling! Garnish with chopped chives and serve!

Harissa Chicken

Net Carbs: 9g / Fiber: 2g / Fat: 61g / Protein: 40g / Calories: 756
Prep time: 20 min / Cooking time: 4 hours / Servings: 4 / Serving size: 1

INGREDIENTS:

- 10 dried chillies
- 5 fresh chillies
- 1tbsp cumin seeds
- 2tsp coriander seeds
- 1tsp caraway seeds
- 4 cloves of garlic
- 2tbsp lemon juice
- 1tbsp apple cider vinegar
- 1 tbsp tomato paste
- 60ml // ¼ cup olive oil
- 900g // 2lb chicken thighs
- 4 red onions
- Salt and pepper

METHOD:

1. To make the harissa paste, blend together all of the ingredients other than the chicken and red onions.

2. Once it's formed a smooth paste, scoop it out of the blender and marinade the chicken with it for 20 minutes.

3. Peel and chop the red onions into quarters. Place in the bottom of your slow cooker and pour over the marinated chicken and harissa paste.

4. Cook at a medium temperature for 4 hours. Serve with salad or your favorite steamed green vegetables.

Chinese Sesame Tofu

Net Carbs: 14g / Fiber: 8g / Fat: 40g / Protein: 42g / Calories: 581
Prep time: 20 min / Cooking time: 1 hour / Servings: 2 / Serving size: 1

INGREDIENTS:

- 4 garlic cloves, minced
- 1tbsp fresh ginger, minced
- 2tbsp tomato paste
- 60ml // ¼ cup soy sauce
- 2tbsp coconut aminos
- 2tsp sesame oil
- 1tsp chilli flakes

- 2 tbsp rice vinegar
- 400g // 14oz tofu
- 225g // 8oz bok choy
- 2tsp sesame seeds
- 50g // 2oz spring onions, as a garnish

METHOD:

1. Make a marinade by mixing together the garlic, ginger, tomato paste, soy sauce, coconut aminos, sesame oil, chilli flakes and rice vinegar. Chop the tofu into small cubes and cover in the marinade. Let the flavors infuse for 20 minutes.

2. Slice the bok choy lengthwise and place the flat side down in your slow cooker. Tip the tofu and marinade on top. Sprinkle with sesame seeds and cook on a medium heat for 1 hour.

3. Serve in a bowl, sprinkled with chopped fresh spring onions.

Fragrant Ginger Chicken

Net Carbs: 2g / Fiber: 0g / Fat: 8g / Protein: 55g / Calories: 314
Prep time: 10 min / Cooking time: 4 hours / Servings: 4 / Serving size: 1

INGREDIENTS:

- 650g // 22oz chicken breast
- 60ml // ¼ cup soy sauce
- 2tbsp lime juice
- 2tsp sesame seeds
- 1tsp lime zest
- 5tsp ginger, grated
- 1 tsp chilli flakes

METHOD:

1. Mix all the ingredients together and leave to marinate.

2. Place in your slow cooker and cook on medium for 4 hours.

3. Serve shredded with salads or your favorite steamed green vegetables.

DINNER

Roast Pork with Creamy Peppercorn Gravy

Net Carbs: 3g / Fiber: 1g / Fat: 51g / Protein: 28g / Calories: 589
Prep time: 15 min / Cooking time: 8 hours / Servings: 6 / Serving size: 1

INGREDIENTS:

- 900g // 2lb pork shoulder
- ½ tsp salt
- 1 bay leaf
- 5 black peppercorns
- 600ml // 2 ½ cups water
- 2 sprigs fresh thyme

- 2 sprigs fresh rosemary
- 2 garlic cloves
- 40g // 1 ½ oz fresh ginger
- 1tbsp smoked paprika powder
- ½ tsp ground black pepper

METHOD:

1. Mince the garlic cloves and ginger and mix with the salt, pepper and paprika to create a paste.

2. Rub the meat with the paste and place in your slow cooker. Add the bay leaf, thyme, rosemary and peppercorns to the pot and pour over the water so that the meat is partially submerged.

3. Cook on a low heat for 8 hours, or overnight.

4. Serve the roast pork with the sauce and your favorite green vegetables.

Peppercorn Gravy

Net Carbs: 1g / Fiber: 1g / Fat: 61g / Protein: 8g / Calories: 243
Prep time: 2 min / Cooking time: 10 minutes / Servings: 6 / Serving size: 1

INGREDIENTS:

♦ 400ml // 2 cups meat drippings

♦ 350ml // 1 ½ cup double cream

♦ 2tsp ground black pepper

METHOD:

1. To make the sauce, remove the meat from the slow cooker and stir the meat juices left in the pot - If it's a little thin you can reduce them further by switching the slow cooker to a high temperature and leaving the lid off for an additional 10 minutes.

2. Once the meat juices are at the desired consistency, swirl in the double cream and stir to combine.

Hungarian Goulash

Net Carbs: 9g / Fiber: 4g / Fat: 36g / Protein: 20g / Calories: 302
Prep time: 10 min / Cooking time: 6 hours / Servings: 8 / Serving size: 1

INGREDIENTS:

- 110g // 4oz butter
- 2 yellow onions
- 2 garlic cloves
- 2 red peppers
- 225g // 8oz celery sticks
- 900g // 2lb beef joint
- 400g // 14oz tinned chopped tomatoes
- 175ml // ⅓ cup water

- 1tbsp tomato paste
- 1tbsp oregano
- 1tbsp paprika
- 1tbsp onion powder
- 1tbsp caraway seeds
- 1 pinch cayenne pepper
- 1 tsp salt
- ¼ tsp black pepper

METHOD:

1. Chop the vegetables into chunky pieces and add to the slow cooker pot.

2. Dice the beef, and mix well with the tomato paste, herbs and seasoning.

3. Add the beef mixture to the pot along with the vegetables. Pour over the water and slow cook for 5-6 hours on a medium temperature.

4. Delicious served with cauliflower rice, butter braised cabbage or just on its own with a dollop of sour cream.

Butter Braised Cabbage

Net Carbs: 6g / Fiber: 2g / Fat: 6g / Protein: 6g / Calories: 113
Prep time: 5 min / Cooking time: 2 hours / Servings: 4 / Serving size: 1

INGREDIENTS:

- ◆ 900g // 2lb green cabbage
- ◆ ½ cup // 4oz butter
- ◆ Salt and pepper

METHOD:

1. Shred the cabbage with a sharp knife.

2. Add to your slow cooker with the butter and cook on a high heat for 2 hours till the cabbage is wilted but still retains some crunch. Season and serve as a side dish accompanying your favorite slow cooker meat dish.

Cheesy Cauliflower Mash

Net Carbs: 10g / Fiber: 7g / Fat: 21g / Protein: 19g / Calories: 320
Prep time: 5 min / Cooking time: 20 minutes / Servings: 4 / Serving size: 1

INGREDIENTS:

- 800g // 28oz cauliflower
- 75g // ½ cup butter
- 75g // ½ cup mature cheddar cheese, grated
- Salt and pepper to taste

METHOD:

1. Chop the cauliflower into small chunks and place in your slow cooker. Add the butter and cheese, season well and cook at a high temperature for 2 hours, or until the cauliflower is soft.

2. Mash with a potato masher and serve as a side dish to your favorite meat dish.

Greek Pesto Chicken with Olives and Feta Cheese

Net Carbs: 6g / Fiber: 2g / Fat: 93g / Protein: 38g / Calories: 1018
Prep time: 5 min / Cooking time: 4 hours / Servings: 4 / Serving size: 1

INGREDIENTS:

- 650g // 1 ½ lb chicken breast, skin still on
- 2tbsp butter
- 3 garlic cloves
- 5tbsp red pesto
- 300ml // 1 ¼ cups double cream
- 75g // 3oz pitted red olives
- 150g // 5oz full-fat feta cheese

METHOD:

1. Use the butter to grease your slow cooker pot. Place the chicken into the pot, skin side up.

2. Crush the garlic cloves and mix with the red pesto and double cream. Pour the mixture over the chicken.

3. Scatter the red pesto, olives and crumbled feta cheese over the top and season the skin of the chicken well with salt and pepper.

4. Bake in your slow cooker for 4 hours at a high temperature. Serve and enjoy with a greek salad.

Keto-friendly Shepherd's Pie

Net Carbs: 6g / Fiber: 5g / Fat: 36g / Protein: 46g / Calories: 620
Prep time: 15 min / Cooking time: 4 hours / Servings: 6 / Serving size: 1

INGREDIENTS:

- 2tbsp butter

- 1 onion

- 1 carrot

- 2 celery sticks

- 4 garlic cloves

- 550g // 1 ¼ lb lamb mince

- 1tsp thyme

- 1tsp rosemary

- 4tbsp tomato paste

- 125ml // ½ cup beef stock

- 225g // 8ozg cottage cheese

- 200g // 7oz grated cheddar cheese

METHOD:

1. Thinly slice the onion, carrot and celery. Mix well with the raw lamb mince and add the dried herbs and seasoning.

2. Stir the tomato paste and butter into the hot beef stock until it is all dissolved. Add this to the lamb and vegetable mixture and mix well till combined.

3. Pour the meat mixture into your slow cooker pot. Spoon dollops of cottage cheese on the top and use a fork to spread around evenly.

4. Top with the grated cheese and bake in your slow cooker for 4 hours at a high heat.

Turnip Gratin

Net carbs: 8g / Fibre: 2g / Fat: 35g / Protein: 11g / Calories: 387
Prep time: 15 min / Cooking time: 4 hours / Servings: 6 / Serving size: 1

INGREDIENTS:

- 2 onion
- 650g // 1 ½ lb turnips
- 1 garlic clove

- 125ml // ½ cup chives, chopped
- 400g // 2 cups double cream
- 200g // 7oz grated cheese

METHOD:

1. Peel the turnips and onions and slice very finely with a mandolin or sharp knife.

2. Grease the inside of your slow cooker pot with a little butter and spoon a dollop of double cream at the bottom of the pot. Slowly layer slices of turnip, onion and double cream until everything is used up. Finish with one last layer of double cream, then sprinkle over the minced garlic, salt and pepper seasoning and grated cheese.

3. Bake in your slow cooker for 4 hours at a high heat, check the turnip is cooked all the way through with a sharp knife before removing from the slow cooker and serving.

Lemon and Caper Chicken Thighs

Net Carbs: 3g / Fiber: 1g / Fat: 54g / Protein: 38g / Calories: 657
Prep time: 10 min / Cooking time: 4 hours / Servings: 4 / Serving size: 1

INGREDIENTS:

- 900g // 31oz chicken thighs
- 2tsp salt
- 1tsp garlic powder
- 1 tsp italian seasoning
- ½ tsp black pepper

- 3tbsp butter
- 2 tbsp lemon juice
- 3tbsp capers
- 1 lemon, sliced into wheels

METHOD:

1. Toss the chicken thighs in the italian seasoning, salt, pepper, lemon juice and garlic powder.

2. Using the butter, grease the insides of the slow cooker pot and place the chicken inside.

3. Place the lemon wheels in and around the chicken pieces, and spoon over the capers.

4. Bake at a medium temperature for 4 hours. Serve with your favorite salad!

Italian Courgette Spaghetti and Meatballs

Net carbs: 7g / Fibre: 4g / Fat: 38g / Protein: 31g / Calories: 504
Prep time: 10 min / Cooking time: 4 hours / Servings: 4 / Serving size: 1

INGREDIENTS:

- 2-3 medium sized courgettes, made into noodles
- 2tbsp olive oil
- 2 tins chopped tomatoes
- 3 garlic cloves, minced
- 2 onions, chopped
- 2tbsp oregano
- 2tsp thyme
- 1tsp rosemary
- 500g // 1lb minced beef
- 1 egg
- 2tbsp almond flour
- 1tsp nutmeg
- Salt and pepper
- Parmesan cheese, to serve

METHOD:

1. First make the sauce by chopping the onion and garlic and mix with the tinned chopped tomatoes and herbs. Pour everything into the bottom of your slow cooker.

2. To make the meatballs - mix the beef mince with the egg, nutmeg and plenty of salt and pepper. Roll into little balls with your hands and coat with a little almond flour to keep them together.

3. Gently arrange the meatballs on top of your sauce in the slow cooker pot. Cook on a medium temperature for 3 and ½ hours, until the meatballs are cooked through and the sauce is thick and bubbling.

4. Make your courgette noodles with the appropriate machine, toss in olive oil and place over the top of your meatballs and sauce. Replace the lid and continue to cook for a further 30 minutes.

5. Once cooked, use tongs to stir the noodles around in the sauce to coat liberally. Serve topped with grated parmesan cheese.

Lamb Stew with Creamy Dill Sauce

Net carbs: 6g / Fibre: 3g / Fat: 49g / Protein: 29g / Calories: 590
Prep time: 10 min / Cooking time: 6 hours / Servings: 6 / Serving size: 1

INGREDIENTS:

- 900g // 2lb lamb cutlets
- 1tsp pepper
- 1tsp salt
- 2 bay leaves
- 250ml // 1 cup fresh dill, chopped
- 2 onions
- 1 carrot
- 1300ml // ¼ cup double cream
- 1tsp white wine vinegar
- 225ml // 1 cup vegetable stock
- 550g // 1 ¼ lb green beans

METHOD:

1. Place the lamb cutlets in the bottom of your slow cooker dish. Scatter the chopped onion and carrot over the top and sprinkle in the chipped dill.

2. Mix the vegetable stock, double cream and white vinegar together. Pour over the meat and vegetables. Add your bay leaves and season well.

3. Wash and trim the green beans and place on top of the lamb casserole mixture.

4. Bake in your slow cooker for 6 hours at a low temperature. Sprinkle with a little more fresh dill and serve.

Mushroom Cauliflower Risotto

Net Carbs: 13g / Fiber: 5g / Fat: 50g / Protein: 15g / Calories: 585
Prep time: 10 min / Cooking time: 3 hours / Servings: 4 / Serving size: 1

INGREDIENTS:

- 1 large cauliflower
- 225ml // 1 cup vegetable stock
- 250g // 9oz mushrooms
- 2 garlic cloves
- 1 onion
- 225ml // 1 cup double cream
- 175ml // ¾ cup dry white wine
- 75g // 2 ½ oz parmesan cheese, grated
- 110g // 4oz butter
- Salt and pepper
- Fresh thyme for garnishing

METHOD:

1. Using the butter, liberally gease your slow cooker pan. Coarsely grate the whole cauliflower into the pan.

2. Thinly slice the mushrooms and onion. Mince the garlic. Add everything to the pot.

3. Pour over the double cream, dry white wine and vegetable stock. Gently stir to incorporate everything. Season well.

4. Cook at a low temperature for 3 hours.

5. Right at the end, stir in the grated parmesan cheese and let simmer for another 10 minutes. The cheese will thicken up your risotto.

6. Garnish with a sprinkle of fresh thyme and serve.

Garlic Parmesan Chicken Wings

Net Carbs: 1g / Fiber: 0g / Fat: 34g / Protein: 27g / Calories: 426
Prep time: 10 min / Cooking time: 4 hours / Servings: 8 / Serving size: 1

INGREDIENTS:

- 1kg // 4lb chicken wings
- 1 tsp salt
- 1 tsp pepper
- 115g // ½ cup butter
- 10 cloves of garlic, minced
- 225g // 1 cup parmesan cheese

METHOD:

1. Mix together the minced garlic, salt, pepper and parmesan cheese.

2. Brush the chicken with a little melted butter and roll each wing in the seasoning.

3. Place in your slow cooker and bake at a high temperature for 4 hours, turning the chicken occasionally so it crisps up on both sides.

BONUS:
28 DAY MEAL PLAN

DAY 1

Breakfast - Smoked Salmon Breakfast Casserole

Net carbs: 6 / Fibre: 1g / Fat: 91g / Protein: 21g / Calories: 890
Prep time: 10 min / Cooking time: 4 hours / Servings: 4 / Serving size: ¼ Slice

INGREDIENTS:

- 275g // 10oz smoked salmon
- 50g // 2oz butter
- 8 eggs
- 225ml // 1 cup double cream
- 150g // 5oz grated cheddar cheese
- A pinch of salt and pepper

METHOD:

1. Whisk together the eggs, double cream, cheese and seasoning. Pour into your greased slow cooker pan.

2. Scatter over pieces of the smoked salmon, poking the pieces down so they are partially submerged in the cheesy egg mixture.

3. Cover and cook on a medium temperature for 3-4 hours until cooked all the way through and golden brown.

4. This breakfast slice can be served hot or cold!

Lunch - Middle Eastern Slow Cooker Beef (See page 36)

Dinner - Roast Pork with Creamy Peppercorn Gravy (See page 48)

DAY 2

Breakfast - Keto Coconut Porridge (See page 22)

Lunch - Creamy Broccoli and Leek Soup
Net carbs: 10g / Fibre: 3g / Fat: 50g / Protein: 15g / Calories:545
Prep time: 7 min / Cooking time: 4 hours / Servings: 4 / Serving size: 1

INGREDIENTS:

- 1 small leek
- 300g // ⅔ lb broccoli
- 475ml // 2 cups water
- 1 vegetable stock cube
- 200g // 7oz cream cheese
- 225ml // 1 cup double cream
- ½ tsp chopped fresh basil
- 1 garlic clove, minced
- Pinch of salt and pepper

METHOD:

1. Wash and chop the leek and broccoli into bite sized chunks.

2. Place the vegetables into your slow cooker, add the water, stock cube, garlic and seasoning.

3. Cook in your slow cooker for 3-4 hours at a high temperature.

4. Pour in the double cream and cream cheese and then stir until fully combined.

5. Use a hand held food processor to blend the soup until it's creamy and smooth with no bits. Serve with a sprinkle of fresh basil.

Dinner - Hungarian Goulash (See page 50)

DAY 3

Breakfast - Bacon and Egg Breakfast Slice (See page 23)

Lunch - BBQ Pulled Pork (See page 37)

Dinner - Korma Chicken Curry

Net carbs: 4g / Fibre: 1g / Fat: 31g / Protein: 34g / Calories: 446
Prep time: 15 min / Cooking time: 6 hours / Servings: 4 / Serving size: 1

INGREDIENTS:

- 4tbsp butter
- 1 red onion
- 110g // 4oz greek yoghurt
- 3 whole cloves
- 1 bay leaf
- 1 cinnamon stick
- 1 star anise
- 3 green cardamom pods
- 8 whole black peppercorns
- 650g // 1 ½ lb chicken breast, thighs or drumsticks
- 1tsp ginger, minced
- 3 garlic cloves, minced

- 1tsp chilli powder
- 1tsp coriander powder
- ½ tsp turmeric
- 1tsp garam masala
- Pinch of salt and pepper
- Fresh coriander to garnish

1. Mix together the greek yoghurt, herbs, spices and seasoning to make a marinade. Toss and liberally coat the chicken in the yoghurt mixture and let it infuse for 20 minutes.

2. Finely chop the onion, garlic and ginger. Use the butter to grease the inside of your slow cooker.

3. Place the marinated chicken, the leftover yogurt mixture and onion, garlic and ginger into your slow cooker.

4. Season well and cook for 6 hours on a medium heat. This is delicious served with cauliflower rice or our keto-friendly flatbread.

DAY 4

Breakfast - Spanish Breakfast Tortillas (See page 24)

Lunch - Stuffed Bell-Pepper Poppers (See page 39)

*Dinner - Greek Pesto Chicken with Olives
and Feta Cheese (See page 53)*

Dessert - Blueberry and Lemon Custard Pudding

Net carbs: 4g / Fibre: 1g / Fat: 17g / Protein: 4g / Calories: 191
Prep time: 15 min / Cooking time: 3 hours / Servings: 12 / Serving size: 1

INGREDIENTS:

- ♦ 6 eggs

- ♦ 400g // ½ cup coconut flour

- ♦ 2 lemons, juice and zest

- ♦ 1tsp liquid stevia sweetener

- ♦ ½ cup confectioners sweetener
  (sugar substitute)

- ♦ ½ tsp salt

- ♦ 400ml // 2 cups double cream

- ♦ 200g // ½ cup blueberries

METHOD:

1. Whisk the eggs whites in a bowl with an electric mixer till they stand up, forming stiff peaks.

2. In a separate bowl, whisk the egg yolks with the cream, salt, lemon juice and zest, sweetener and coconut flour until they are smooth and fully incorporated.

3. Carefully fold the stiff egg whites into the yolk mixture. Grease your slow cooker and add the mixture to the pot.

4. Scatter over the blueberries, cover and cook on a low temperature for 3 hours or until a toothpick comes out clean.

5. Allow the cake to cool, slice and serve with a dollop of whipped cream.

DAY 5

Breakfast - Cheesy Slow Cooker Scrambled Eggs

Net carbs: 2g / Fibre: 0g / Fat: 40g / Protein: 15g / Calories: 400
Prep time: 3 min / Cooking time: 2 hours / Servings: 2 / Serving size: 1

INGREDIENTS:

- 50g // 2oz butter, melted
- 4 eggs
- 15g // 0.5oz cheddar cheese
- chopped fresh herbs, such as chives or parsley
- pinch of sea salt and pepper

METHOD:

1. Whisk together eggs, melted butter, cheese, herbs and seasoning.

2. Place in your slow cooker and cook on medium heat for 2 hours.

3. When cooked, use a fork to mix and mash up the eggs. Don't worry if they're a little runny in the middle still, you can leave them in the slow cooker for a further 10 minutes to firm up.

Lunch - Hearty Chicken Soup (See page 40)

Dinner - Keto-friendly Shepherd's Pie (See page 54)

DAY 6

Breakfast - Stewed Summer Berries with Yoghurt (See page 25)

Lunch - Tomato and Parmasan Soup

Net carbs: 3g / Fibre: 1g / Fat: 12g / Protein: 6g / Calories: 146
Prep time: 5 min / Cooking time: 15 min / Servings: 12 / Serving size: 1

INGREDIENTS:

- 2tbsp butter
- 110g // 4oz red onion
- 2 garlic cloves
- 1tbsp dried basil
- 1tsp dried oregano
- 225g // 8oz sour cream
- 1l // 4 cups chicken stock
- 2 cans of chopped tomatoes
- 150g // 5oz grated parmesan
- 1tsp salt
- 1tsp black pepper
- 4-6 fresh basil leaves as a garnish

METHOD:

1. Finely slice the onion and garlic and add to the slow cooker.

2. Sprinkle over the herbs and pour in the chopped tomatoes, chicken stock and butter. Season well with salt and pepper.

3. Cook in your slow cooker for 2 hours on a high heat.

4. Open the lid and pour in the sour cream. Using a hand held food processor, blend the soup till smooth.

5. Serve with a sprinkle of parmesan cheese and basil leaves as a garnish.

Dinner - Turnip Gratin (See page 56)

DAY 7

Breakfast - Sausage and Egg Bake (See page 26)

Lunch - Warm Broccoli Salad (See page 41)

Dinner - Bangers with Cheesy Cauliflower Mash
Net carbs: 12g / Fibre: 5g / Fat: 115g / Protein: 46g / Calories: 1276
Prep time: 5 min / Cooking time: 2 hours / Servings: 4 / Serving size: 1

INGREDIENTS:

- 650g // 1.4lb good quality, gluten-free pork sausages
- 3 onions, sliced
- 1tbsp olive oil
- 4 servings of our cheesy cauliflower mash (see recipes)

METHOD:

1. Place sausages and sliced onions in your slow cooker, drizzle with olive oil and bake for 2 hours at a high temperature.

2. Serve with our cheesy cauliflower mash and your favorite gluten-free gravy.

DAY 8

Breakfast - Breakfast Shakshuka (See page 27)

Lunch - Tuna Steak Cheese Melt (See page 42)

Dinner - Lemon and Caper Chicken Thighs (See page 57)

Snack - Chicken Wings with Chipotle Aioli

Net carbs: 2g / Fibre: 1g / Fat: 42g / Protein: 42g / Calories: 569
Prep time: 10 min / Cooking time: 4 hours / Servings: 4 / Serving size: 1

INGREDIENTS:

- 900g // 2lb chicken wings (or thighs/ drumsticks)
- 2tbsp olive oil
- 2tbsp tomato paste
- 1tsp salt
- 1tsp paprika powder
- 1tbsp chipotle tabasco
- 3 tbsp mayonnaise

METHOD:

1. Mix together the olive oil, tomato paste, salt, paprika and tabasco to make a paste. Coat the chicken wings liberally in marinade and set to one side to infuse for 10 minutes.

2. Place in your slow cooker and bake for 4 hours at a high temperature.

3. Mix together 1 tsp of chipotle tabasco with the mayonnaise to create an easy dipping sauce.

DAY 9

Breakfast - Giant Breakfast Muffin
Net carbs: 2g / Fibre: 0g / Fat: 26g / Protein: 23g / Calories: 336
Prep time: 5 min / Cooking time: 4 hours / Servings: 6 / Serving size: 1

INGREDIENTS:

- 2 spring onions, sliced finely
- 150g // 5oz chorizo sausage
- 12 eggs
- 2tbsp red pesto
- 180g // 6oz grated cheese
- Salt and pepper

METHOD:

1. Chop and dice the chorizo sausage and spring onions.

2. Whisk together the eggs, half of the cheese and the seasoning.

3. Pour the cheesy egg mixture into a greased slow cooker and scatter the chorizo and spring onion on top.

4. Dollop blobs of red pesto over the top and scatter with the remaining cheese.

5. Cook in your slow cooker for 4 hours. Slice into quarters and serve!

Lunch - Cheesy Philly-Cheesesteak Soup (See page 43)

Dinner - Italian Courgette Spaghetti and Meatballs (See page 58)

DAY 10

Breakfast - Scrambled Tofu with Chives (See page 29)

Lunch - Spinach Frittata

Net carbs: 4g / Fibre: 1g / Fat: 59g / Protein: 27g / Calories: 661
Prep time: 10 min / Cooking time: 4 hours / Servings: 4 / Serving size: 1 Slice

INGREDIENTS:

- 150g //5oz chorizo sausage
- 2tbsp butter
- 225g // 8oz spinach
- 8 eggs
- 225ml // 1 cup double cream
- 150g // 5oz grated cheddar cheese
- Pinch of salt and pepper

METHOD:

1. Chop the chorizo into small chunks and set aside.

2. Whisk the eggs, butter, double cream and half of the cheese in a bowl. Grease the inside of your slow cooker and pour in the creamy egg mixture.

3. Tip in the spinach and poke it down so that it is fully submerged in the egg. Scatter the sliced chorizo on top, then sprinkle the remaining cheese on the top.

4. Cook at a medium heat for 4 hours. Cut into slices and serve your frittata hot or cold.

Dinner - Lamb Stew with Creamy Dill Sauce (See page 60)

DAY 11

Breakfast - Courgette Breakfast Loaf with Butter (See page 30)

Lunch - Harissa Chicken (See page 44)

Dinner - Roast Chicken with Garlic and Herb Butter

Net carbs: 0.3g / Fibre: 0g / Fat: 82g / Protein: 58g / Calories: 984
Prep time: 25 min / Cooking time: 6 hours / Servings: 4 / Serving size: 1

INGREDIENTS:

- 1.5kg // 3lb whole chicken
- 150g // 5oz butter
- 4 cloves of garlic, minced
- 2 sprigs of fresh thyme
- 1 sprig fresh rosemary
- Salt and pepper to taste
- 2 yellow onions, cut into quarters
- Pinch of salt and pepper

METHOD:

1. First, mix the butter, minced garlic and herbs into a paste.

2. Place the whole chicken into your slow cooker and liberally cover with the herb butter. Scatter chunks of the onion in the bottom of the dish and season liberally with salt and pepper.

3. Bake for 6 hours in your slow cooker, constantly basting with the melted garlic and herb butter to keep the chicken moist.

DAY 12

Breakfast - Keto Spiced Chai 'Oatmeal' (See page 31)

Lunch - Chinese Sesame Tofu (See page 45)

Dinner - Mushroom Cauliflower Risotto (See page 61)

Dessert - Stewed Berry Compote with Whipped Cream

Net carbs: 6g / Fibre: 5g / Fat: 29g / Protein: 3g / Calories: 307
Prep time: 15 min / Cooking time: 3 hours / Servings: 2 / Serving size: 1

INGREDIENTS:

- 150g // 5oz fresh berries, such as raspberries, strawberries or blueberries
- 1 tsp cinnamon
- 1 star anise
- 1 lemon, zest and juice
- 150ml // ⅔ cup double cream
- ¼ tsp vanilla essence
- Bunch of fresh mint as a garnish

METHOD:

1. Place the berries, cinnamon, star anise, lemon juice and zest in your slow cooker. Cook on a low heat for 3 hours.

2. Whip the cream and vanilla essence together with an electric mixer, till it forms stiff peaks.

3. To serve, transfer the berry compote into a bowl, dollop with vanilla cream and garnish with mint.

DAY 13

Breakfast - Mexican Breakfast Slice

Net Carbs: 3g / Fiber: 1g / Fat: 23g / Protein: 15g / Calories: 284
Prep time: 5 min / Cooking time: 5 hours / Servings: 1 / Serving size: 1 slice

INGREDIENTS:

- 650g // 1 ½ lb minced pork
- ½ tsp garlic powder
- ½ tsp coriander
- 1 tsp cumin
- 1 tsp chilli powder
- ¼ tsp salt
- 1 cup chopped tinned tomatoes
- 1 onion
- 10 eggs
- 225ml // 1 cup double cream
- 225g // 1 cup grated cheese

1. In a frying pan, brown off the pork mince and add the diced onion and chopped tomatoes, garlic powder, coriander, cumin, chilli and salt. Simmer gently to thicken the sauce.

2. Whisk the eggs with the double cream. Grease the inside of your slow cooker and pour in in the egg mixture.

3. Spoon over ladles of the pork and sauce mixture. Top with grated cheese.

4. Cook on low in the slow cooker for 5 hours. Gently slice the egg mixture to check it's cooked all the way through and fluffy. Serve warm or cold for a quick and easy breakfast.

Lunch - Fragrant Ginger Chicken (See page 46)

Dinner - Garlic Parmesan Chicken Wings (See page 63)

DAY 14

Breakfast - Slow Cooker Keto Cinnamon Swirl Cake (See page 32)

Lunch - Slow Cooker Caribbean Chicken

Net Carbs: 9g / Fiber: 4g / Fat: 99g / Protein: 65g / Calories: 986
Prep time: 8 min / Cooking time: 5 hours / Servings: 6 / Serving size: 1

INGREDIENTS:

- 1.5kg // 3lb chicken on the bone - legs, wings and thighs
- 225ml // 1 cup full fat greek yoghurt
- 5 lime leaves

- 1tbsp coriander seeds
- 1tbso ground ginger
- ½ tsp black pepper
- 2tsp salt
- Juice of 2 limes

METHOD:

1. Mix the coriander seeds, ginger, lime juice and seasoning with the yoghurt. Pour the mixture over the chicken and marinate for 1 hour.

2. Transfer the chicken to the slow cooker and cook on high for 3-4 hours on a high heat.

3. Serve the chicken with your favorite salad or braised veggies!

Dinner - Hungarian Goulash (See page 50)

DAY 15

Breakfast - Keto Coconut Porridge (See page 22)

Lunch - Middle Eastern Slow Cooker Beef (See page 36)

Dinner - Parisian Beef Bourguignon

Net Carbs: 13g / Fiber: 5g / Fat: 71g / Protein: 38g / Calories: 933
Prep time: 10 min / Cooking time: 8 hours / Servings: 6 / Serving size: 1

INGREDIENTS:

- ♦ 75g // 3oz butter

- ♦ 600g // 1 ⅓ lbs beef joint

- ♦ 150g // 5oz smoky bacon strips

- ♦ 75g // 3oz shallot onions

- ♦ 3 garlic cloves

- ♦ 1 carrot

- ♦ 75g // 3oz button mushrooms

- ♦ 475ml // 2 cups dry red wine

- ♦ 2 bay leaves

- ♦ 1 tsp thyme

- ♦ Salt and pepper to taste

1. Chop the beef and streaky bacon into small chunks and place in the bottom of your slow cooker.

2. Dice the carrot, chop the mushrooms into quarters and half the shallot onions. Peel and roughly crush the garlic cloves. Scatter the vegetables over the meat in the bottom of the slow cooker.

3. Pour over the red wine and place the bay leaves and thyme in the pot. Season well with salt and pepper.

4. Cook on a low heat for 6-8 hours, or longer if your cut of beef is a little on the tough side. Serve with buttery braised cabbage and cauliflower mash!

DAY 16

Breakfast - Bacon and Egg Breakfast Slice (See page 23)

Lunch - BBQ Pulled Pork (See page 37)

Dinner - Roast Pork with Creamy Peppercorn Gravy (See page 48)

Snack - Boiled Eggs with Peppery Mayonnaise

Net carbs: 1g / Fibre: 1g / Fat: 29g / Protein:11g / Calories: 316
Prep time: 2 min / Cooking time: 2-5 hours / Servings: 2 / Serving size: 1

INGREDIENTS:

- ♦ 8 eggs
- ♦ 8tbsp mayonnaise
- ♦ Pinch of salt and pepper

METHOD:

1. Fill your slow cooker with water and set to a high temperature.

2. Place the 8 eggs into the water and cook for between 2-5 hours, depending on how runny you like your yolks.

3. Once cooked, remove your eggs and run them under some cold water to cool.

4. Peel the eggs, slice in half and drizzle liberally with your mayonnaise and cracked black pepper.

DAY 17

Breakfast - Mexican Breakfast Eggs

Net carbs: 12g / Fibre: 7g / Fat: 46g / Protein: 17g / Calories: 542
Prep time: 10 min / Cooking time: 4 hours / Servings: 4 / Serving size: 1

INGREDIENTS:

- 125ml // ½ cup olive oil
- 1 white onion
- 2 garlic cloves
- 2 fresh jalapenos
- 475ml // 2 cups canned diced tomatoes
- 6 eggs
- 50g // 2oz grated cheese
- 4 tbsp chopped coriander
- 1 avocado
- Pinch of salt and pepper

METHOD:

1. Chop the onion, garlic and jalapenos and mix together. Place in your slow cooker.

2. Pour over the chopped tomatoes and stir to combine. Season with a little salt and pepper.

3. Cook the sauce in your slow cooker for 4 hours at a high temperature.

4. Once cooked, use a spoon to make little well's on the top of the thick sauce. Crack each egg into the sauce, top with cheese and cook for a further 30 minutes on a high heat till the eggs have poached and the cheese has melted.

5. Serve sprinkled with chopped fresh coriander and a slice or two of our keto-friendly flatbread.

Lunch - Stuffed Bell-Pepper Poppers (See page 39)

*Dinner - Greek Pesto Chicken with Olives
and Feta Cheese (See page 53)*

DAY 18

Breakfast - Spanish Breakfast Tortillas (See page 24)

Breakfast - Spanish Breakfast Tortillas (See page 24)

Lunch - Turkey Chilli Hot-Pot

Net Carbs: 19g / Fiber: 6g / Fat: 48g / Protein: 36g / Calories: 649
Prep time: 3 min / Cooking time: 4 hours / Servings: 6 / Serving size: 1

INGREDIENTS:

- 60ml // ¼ cup olive oil
- 650g // 1 ½ lbs ground turkey mince
- 4 garlic cloves
- 3 onions
- 425g // 15oz tinned chopped tomatoes
- 225ml // 1 cup hot water
- 175g // 6oz tomato paste
- 2tbsp hot chilli powder
- 2tbsp smoked paprika
- 2tsp cumin seeds
- Salt and pepper to taste

METHOD:

1. Slice the onions and mince the garlic. Scatter over the bottom of the slow cooker and add the turkey mince.

2. Mix together the chilli powder, cumin seeds, paprika, salt and pepper. Sprinkle over the mince and onion mix.

3. In a jug, mix the hot water, tinned tomatoes, olive oil and tomato paste until combined.

4. Pour over the meat and cook for 3-4 hours on a high heat until your turkey chilli is bubbling and thick.

5. Serve with a dollop of sour cream or grated cheese, and a scattering of fresh coriander! You could also use leftovers from this meal to make wraps with salad, avocado and our keto friendly flatbread.

Dinner - Keto-friendly Shepherd's Pie (See page 54)

DAY 19

Breakfast - Stewed Summer Berries with Yoghurt (See page 25)

Lunch - Hearty Chicken Soup (See page 40)

Dinner - Farmhouse Venison Stew

Net Carbs: 11g / Fiber: 3g / Fat: 47g / Protein: 32g / Calories: 598
Prep time: 10 min / Cooking time: 6 hours / Servings: 6 / Serving size: 1

INGREDIENTS:

- ◆ 4tbsp olive oil
- ◆ 800g // 1 ¾ lbs venison
- ◆ 1 carrot
- ◆ 1 onion
- ◆ 2 garlic cloves
- ◆ 1tbsp soy sauce
- ◆ 225ml // 1 cup double cream
- ◆ 1 sprig fresh rosemary
- ◆ 4 sprigs fresh thyme
- ◆ 1tsp paprika
- ◆ 4 dried juniper berries
- ◆ 2tbsp butter
- ◆ Salt and black pepper to taste

METHOD:

1. Dice the venison into bite size chunks and place in the bottom of the slow cooker. Season well and throw in the juniper berries and fresh herbs.

2. Dice the carrot and onion. Crush the garlic cloves. Scatter everything on top of the meat in the slow cooker and add spices.

3. Pour in the soy sauce and add the butter and olive oil. Cook on a low heat for 5 hours until the meat is tender and bubbling.

4. Add the double cream and stir to incorporate. Cook for an additional 1 hour once the cream has been added. Serve with buttery cauliflower mash or your favorite green vegetables.

DAY 20

Breakfast - Sausage and Egg Bake (See page 26)

Lunch - Warm Broccoli Salad (See page 41)

Dinner - Turnip Gratin (See page 56)

Dessert - Baked Peaches with Cream

Net carbs: 11g / Fibre: 2g / Fat: 27g / Protein: 3g / Calories: 298
Prep time: 15 min / Cooking time: 2 hours / Servings: 4 / Serving size: 1

INGREDIENTS:

- 4 ripe peaches
- 1tsp cinnamon
- 2tbsp coconut oil
- 225ml // 1 cup double cream, whipped
- Sprigs of mint to garnish

METHOD:

1. Slice the peaches in half and remove the stones. Slice into chunky segments.

2. Place the peaches in the bottom of your slow cooker and drizzle over the coconut oil. Sprinkle over the cinnamon.

3. Cook on high for 2 hours, remove from the slow cooker and serve warm with the whipped double cream and a few mint leaves.

DAY 21

Breakfast - Mushroom and Bacon Slice

Net carbs: 6 / Fibre: 1g / Fat: 81g / Protein: 31g / Calories: 876
Prep time: 10 min / Cooking time: 4 hours / Servings: 4 / Serving size: ¼ Slice

INGREDIENTS:

- 175g // 6oz mushrooms
- 275g // 10oz streaky bacon
- 50g // 2oz butter
- 8 eggs
- 225ml // 1 cup double cream
- 150g // 5oz grated cheddar cheese
- 1tsp onion powder
- A pinch of salt and pepper

METHOD:

1. Slice up the mushrooms and bacon into chunky strips.

2. Whisk together the eggs, double cream, cheese and onion powder.

3. Sprinkle in the mushrooms and bacon and arrange evenly in the greased slow cooker pan, and season with the salt and pepper.

4. Pour over your egg mixture, cover and cook on a medium temperature for 3-4 hours until cooked all the way through and golden brown.

5. This breakfast slice can be served hot or cold!

Lunch - Tuna Steak Cheese Melt (See page 42)

Dinner - Lemon and Caper Chicken Thighs (See page 57)

DAY 22

Breakfast - Breakfast Shakshuka (See page 27)

Lunch - Baked Salmon with Pesto

Net carbs: 3g / Fibre: 1g / Fat: 88g / Protein: 52g / Calories: 1025
Prep time: 5 min / Cooking time: 3 hours / Servings: 4 / Serving size: 1

INGREDIENTS:

- 900g // 2lb salmon fillet
- 4tbsp green pesto

- Pinch of salt and pepper

Sauce:

- 4tbsp green pesto
- 225ml // 1 cup mayonnaise

- Pinch of salt and pepper

METHOD:

1. Place the salmon skin side down in the greased slow cooker pan. Season the fish and spread a little green pesto on the top. Drizzle with olive oil.

2. Cook in your slow cooker on a high temperature for 2-3 hours until the pesto on the top is looking browned and a little crispy.

3. For the sauce, mix together the rest of the ingredients in a bowl until smooth and creamy.

4. Spoon over the fish and serve!

Dinner - Italian Courgette Spaghetti and Meatballs (See page 58)

DAY 23

Breakfast - Scrambled Tofu with Chives (See page 29)

Lunch - Cheesy Philly-Cheesesteak Soup (See page 43)

Dinner - Curried Lamb Stew

Net Carbs: 16g / Fiber: 8g / Fat: 44g / Protein: 33g / Calories: 610
Prep time: 10 min / Cooking time: 10 hours / Servings: 8 / Serving size: 1

INGREDIENTS:

- 900g // 6lb lamb shoulder

- 3 onions

- 1 carrot

- 2 celery sticks

- 1 red chilli

- 4 cloves of garlic

- 2tbsp curry powder

- 1tsp sea salt

- 50g // 2oz butter or ghee

- 400g // 14oz tinned chopped tomatoes

- 60ml // ¼ cup water

1. Finely chop the onion, carrot and celery sticks. Mince together the red chilli and garlic.

2. Chop the lamb into small bite-sized pieces and add to the slow cooker. Scatter the vegetables and minced chilli and garlic over the top. Sprinkle with curry powder, add the butter and season well.

3. Pour over the water and chopped tomatoes and mix lightly with a wooden spoon so that everything is nicely combined.

4. Cook on low in your slow cooker for 8-10 hours. The lamb will be beautifully tender and the curry sauce will be thick and rich. Serve with keto flatbread and a dollop of sour cream.

DAY 24

Breakfast - Courgette Breakfast Loaf with Butter (See page 30)

Lunch - Harissa Chicken (See page 44)

Dinner - Lamb Stew with Creamy Dill Sauce (See page 60)

Snack - Bacon Wrapped Halloumi Sticks

Net carbs: 4g / Fibre: 0g / Fat: 61g / Protein: 34g / Calories: 705
Prep time: 10 min / Cooking time: 2 hours / Servings: 2 / Serving size: 1

INGREDIENTS:

- ◆ 225g // 8oz halloumi cheese
- ◆ 175g // 6oz streaky bacon

METHOD:

1. Slice your block of halloumi cheese into neat little sticks. Wrap with the streaky bacon and place in the bottom of your slow cooker.

2. Bake for 2 hours at a high temperature, turning occasionally to crisp up the bacon.

3. Serve as a snack, with your favorite creamy dip!

DAY 25

Breakfast - Spanish Eggs

Net carbs: 2g / Fibre: 1g / Fat: 15g / Protein: 19g / Calories: 140
Prep time: 5 min / Cooking time: 4 hours / Servings: 3 / Serving size: 1

INGREDIENTS:

- 75g // 3oz chorizo sausage
- 75g // 3oz grated mozzarella cheese
- 6 large eggs
- 10 cherry tomatoes, halved
- 4tsp red pesto
- Pinch of salt and pepper

METHOD:

1. Chop the chorizo sausage into thin slices. Slice the cherry tomatoes in half.

2. Whisk the eggs with half the mozzarella cheese and the pesto.

3. Pour the egg mixture into your greased slow cooker pan and scatter the sliced chorizo and cherry tomatoes over the top.

4. Season well with salt and pepper and cook for 4 hours at a medium temperature.

Lunch - Chinese Sesame Tofu (See page 45)

Dinner - Mushroom Cauliflower Risotto (See page 61)

DAY 26

Breakfast - Keto Spiced Chai 'Oatmeal' (See page 31)

Lunch - Chunky Chicken and Vegetable Soup
Net Carbs: 10g / Fiber: 11g / Fat: 38g / Protein: 39g / Calories: 548
Prep time: 10 min / Cooking time: 5 hours / Servings: 6 / Serving size: 1 cup

INGREDIENTS:

- 2tbsp butter
- 200g // 7oz celery sticks
- 110g // 4oz onion
- 2 garlic cloves
- 1tsp fresh thyme
- 1tsp salt
- ½ tsp black pepper
- 750g // 1 ⅔ lbs boneless chicken breast or thighs
- 1.2l // 5 cups chicken stock
- 1 green pepper
- 200g // 7oz courgette
- 400g // 14 oz cauliflower
- bunch of fresh parsley for garnishing

METHOD:

1. Chop and dice the vegetables and slice the chicken into thin strips. Mince the garlic into a paste.

2. Place the butter, garlic, vegetables and chicken into the slow cooker and pour over the chicken stock and fresh thyme, black pepper and salt.

3. Cook in your slow cooker overnight, or minimum 4-5 hours on a medium temperature.

4. Serve the soup in bowls or mugs with a sprinkle of chopped parsley and additional salt and pepper to taste.

Dinner - Garlic Parmesan Chicken Wings (See page 63)

DAY 27

Breakfast - Slow Cooker Keto Cinnamon Swirl Cake (See page 32)

Lunch - Fragrant Ginger Chicken (See page 46)

Dinner - Asian Style Sticky Orange Pork

Net Carbs: 5g / Fiber: 1g / Fat: 21g / Protein: 31g / Calories: 34
Prep time: 10 min / Cooking time: 8 hours / Servings: 6 / Serving size: 1

INGREDIENTS:

- 2tbsp bacon fat or lard
- 900g // 2lb pork ribs
- ¼ tsp salt
- ¼ tsp pepper
- 1 onion
- 1 ½ tsp ginger
- 3 garlic cloves
- 1 tbsp chinese five spice
- 2tbsp orange zest
- 60ml // ⅓ cup fresh squeezed orange juice
- 75ml // ⅓ cup rice vinegar
- 75ml // 3oz soy sauce
- ½ tsp fish sauce
- 175g // 6oz meat stock

METHOD:

1. Slice the onion and mince the garlic and ginger. Mix with the orange juice and zest, vinegar, soy sauce, fish sauce, meat stock and chinese 5 spice seasoning.

2. Put the pork ribs in the slow cooker and pour over the seasoning paste. Add the bacon fat or lard.

3. Pour over the hot meat stock and slow cook for 6-8 hours until the meat is falling off the bone.

4. Once cooked you can shred the meat with two forks and serve with your favorite asian style stir-fry vegetables or cauliflower rice.

DAY 28

Breakfast - Breakfast Shakshuka (See page 27)

Lunch - Hearty Chicken Soup (See page 40)

Dinner - Stuffed Bell-Pepper Poppers (See page 39)

Dessert - Summer Fruits Crumble

Net carbs: 5g / Fibre: 8g / Fat: 27g / Protein: 7g / Calories: 315
Prep time: 5 min / Cooking time: 3 hours / Servings: 4 / Serving size: 1

INGREDIENTS:

- 275g // 10oz fresh berries, such as blueberries, strawberries and raspberries
- 2tbsp lime juice
- 60g // 2oz pecan nuts, hazelnuts or almonds (or a mixture of all three)
- 15g // ½ oz shredded coconut
- 75g // ½ cup sunflower seeds
- ½ cinnamon powder
- 30g // ¼ cup almond flour

METHOD:

1. Place the berries and lime juice in the bottom of your greased slow cooker.

2. Mix together the dry ingredients and sprinkle over the top to form the crumble.

3. Cook in your slow cooker for 3 hours at a high temperature.

Printed in Great Britain
by Amazon